# Becoming a
# New Manager

# Pocket Mentor Series

The *Pocket Mentor* Series offers immediate solutions to common challenges managers face on the job every day. Each book in the series is packed with handy tools, self-tests, and real-life examples to help you identify your strengths and weaknesses and hone critical skills. Whether you're at your desk, in a meeting, or on the road, these portable guides enable you to tackle the daily demands of your work with greater speed, savvy, and effectiveness.

**Books in the series:**

*Leading Teams*

*Running Meetings*

*Managing Time*

*Managing Projects*

*Coaching People*

*Giving Feedback*

*Leading People*

*Negotiating Outcomes*

*Writing for Business*

*Giving Presentations*

*Understanding Finance*

*Dismissing an Employee*

*Creating a Business Plan*

*Managing Stress*

*Delegating Work*

*Shaping Your Career*

*Persuading People*

*Managing Crises*

*Managing Up*

*Becoming a New Manager*

# Becoming a New Manager

## Expert Solutions to Everyday Challenges

**Harvard Business Press**

Boston, Massachusetts

No part of this publication may be reproduced, stored in or introduced into a re-trieval system, or transmitted, in any form, or by any means (electronic, mechanical, photocopying, recording, or otherwise), without the prior permission of the pub-lisher. Requests for permission should be directed to permissions@hbsp.harvard.edu, or mailed to Permissions, Harvard Business School Publishing, 60 Harvard Way, Boston, Massachusetts 02163.

**Library of Congress Cataloging-in-Publication Data**

Becoming a new manager : expert solutions to everyday challenges.
    p. cm. — (Pocket mentor series)
  Includes bibliographical references.
  ISBN 978-1-4221-2507-6
  1. Management.  2. Executive ability.  3. Supervision of employees.
  HD31.B3699543 2008
  658—dc22

                                        2008023284

The paper used in this publication meets the requirements of the American National Standard for Permanence of Paper for Publications and Documents in Libraries and Archives Z39.48-1992.

# Contents

## Defining Your New Role    21

*Explanations of three crucial parts of your new role.*

## Managing Teams    27

*Insights into how teams are beneficial and how to manage them effectively.*

## Managing Individual Employees    31

*Strategies for getting the most from your direct reports.*

## Promoting Diversity and Group Culture    39

*Suggestions for leveraging differences and crafting a productive culture in your group.*

## Embracing Your New Identity    45

*Helpful ideas for adjusting to the new person you'll become as a manager.*

## Strengthening Your Emotional Intelligence    51

*Ideas for using "EI" to benefit your group and yourself.*

## Coping with New Feelings    55

*Strategies for dealing with the emotions that can come with being a manager.*

# Mentor's Message: A Challenging and Rewarding Journey

You've just been promoted to a managerial position, after years of excelling as an individual contributor. While you're excited by the new opportunity to come, you're also a bit nervous about taking on new challenges and operating in a very different role from what you're used to.

All of these mixed feelings are normal. They're also signs of wisdom. The fact that you're feeling this way suggests that you're aware that transitioning into management is both a challenging and rewarding journey—one that takes time, patience, and practice.

So, as you look ahead to your new role, get ready to set aside what you have assumed about what it means to be a manager, because the realities may catch you by surprise. And prepare to master a new set of skills, including leading teams, balancing conflicting expectations from various stakeholders, and shaping the culture of your department or group.

This guide introduces you to the truths about managerial work and provides suggestions and tools that will help you make valuable contributions to your organization as you transition into the managerial role.

*Linda A. Hill, Mentor*

From her more than twenty years of extensive field work, Professor Linda A. Hill has helped managers create the conditions for effective management in today's flatter and increasingly diverse organizations. She is a professor and chair of the Leadership Initiative at Harvard Business School. She is also the author of the best-selling *Becoming a Manager* (Harvard Business School Press, 2003) and the content expert for *Coaching for Results and Managing Direct Reports*, award-winning interactive programs from Harvard Business School Publishing.

# Becoming a New Manager: The Basics

# Understanding
# Myths About
# Management

CONGRATULATIONS—YOU'RE BECOMING a manager! You've worked hard, and now you're preparing to take a big step into a new role. Perhaps you're entering the realm of management from any of these directions:

- You've scored impressive achievements as an individual contributor—for example, as a top engineer for your company.

- Your supervisor has promoted you to a team-leadership position—for instance, head of a product-development team.

- You've built a successful one-person business of your own. To sustain that success, you now need to hire and manage staff for the first time, such as an administrative assistant, a bookkeeper, or salespeople.

Wherever you're coming from, you can boost your chances of continued success in your new role by understanding what managers really do. To begin, let's consider a number of all-too-common myths about management—and replace them with their corresponding truths.

## "I'll use the same skills as before"

Many new managers believe they'll be using the same skills they used as individual contributors—except that they'll need to apply those skills to more challenging projects. But *in reality*, the skills that lead to success as an individual contributor differ markedly from those needed to manage.

For example, suppose you're being promoted from salesperson to regional sales manager. As a salesperson, you probably possessed a number of essential, specific skills, including understanding the features and benefits of the product you were selling, knowing how to identify and fulfill customers' needs through your company's offerings, and making sales calls on your own.

As a regional sales manager, you still need to use the skills you honed as an individual salesperson, but now you also need to work through others to achieve your objectives. New managerial skills will be more people- and process-oriented than before as you:

- Travel with your salespeople to observe their selling styles

- Coach newly hired members of your sales team

- Assess each of your direct reports' performance

- Work with peers to acquire necessary resources for your team

- Motivate salespeople to achieve the company's regional sales objectives

The skills you bring to your new position will remain valuable throughout your career. However, your success as a manager will also depend on a different set of skills—particularly people skills.

## "I'll have power"

Do you imagine that, as a manager, you'll have more power than you had as an individual contributor? It's easy to reach this conclusion. After all, many managers have more formal *authority*, in the form of control over budgets, staffing, and other aspects of their group. And they have higher *status* within the organization. They also have more *access* to important organizational resources, such as their own supervisors' advice and support, the attention of top-level executives, training and development opportunities, and so forth.

Managers do have power, but *in reality*, power does not guarantee that a manager has influence. As a manager, you have to use the tools of power—authority, status, and access—to *influence* others. But power and influence are two different things.

---

**POWER** *n* 1: An individual's or group's *potential* to influence another individual or group.

---

**INFLUENCE** *n* 1: The *exercising* of power to change an individual's or group's behavior, attitudes, and values.

---

The amount of power and influence you accumulate stems from two sources:

1. **Your position in the organization.** Your position in your organization's hierarchy affects your ability to influence others. For example, if you have a central or highly visible position in your organization, then you have more power than if your position is more marginal. A marketing manager overseeing the mar-

keting plan for the company's most profitable product would likely have more positional power than a manager in the field who is responsible for a product in a maturing market.

2. **Your personal characteristics.** You gain power from your expertise, understanding, effort, reliability, and charisma. If people perceive that you are knowledgeable, hardworking, and trustworthy, they are more likely to follow your lead or to be influenced by you. For example, if your team members know that you keep track of how they are doing on a project, and you get the help and resources they need to do their job, they are likely to work hard for the best end results.

In developing positional power, remember the *Manager's Law of Reciprocity*: to influence others to help you get things done, provide them with valued resources and services in exchange for resources and services *you* need. There are many kinds of valued resources and services to offer: for example, sharing knowledge and information, offering aid or advice, acknowledging and accepting other people's contributions.

Though much of your managerial power may derive from the daily activities you perform and your location within the organization, it's your *personal attributes* and behaviors that most determine how well you capitalize on your position. How do you leverage your personal attributes? You cultivate networks of mutually beneficial relationships with people whose cooperation you need to succeed. To develop such networks, you need to keep a basic law of human nature in mind: what goes around comes around.

## "I'll have a lot more freedom"

Many new managers believe they'll have far more freedom to make decisions and take action than they had as individual contributors. Some may also assume that they'll have more free time than before, because they'll have direct reports to handle a lot of the work that needs doing. *In reality*, managers have far *less* freedom (and free time!) to act alone than they might have anticipated. That's because they need the cooperation of other people to get things done—including peers, supervisors, direct reports, and others *within* the organization, as well as customers, suppliers, competitors, and others *outside* the organization. Thus, managers depend on a network of other people to accomplish their goals, a network they must spend time developing and maintaining.

Managers assume a whole new set of duties, obligations, and relationships. For example, if you are a new manager of customer service, you'll have to make sure that your group's efforts coincide with the organization's overall marketing and strategic plan. If customer service is a top priority, then your managerial role becomes critical for the success of the company.

## "I'll always have control"

Many managers may seem to have mastered their positions, and their outward appearance can be convincing—even intimidating—to their direct reports or peers. But all managers are human, and *in reality*, even the most self-assured have their moments of frustration and feelings of uncertainty.

As a new manager, you need to recognize that moments of frustration are normal. Occasionally, you will certainly feel constrained, uncertain about your ability to handle the job, and stressed about leading others. You may also feel frustrated when direct reports don't take your direction or listen to you, and annoyed or discouraged by all the "politicking" you need to do to build influence and get work done.

Remember: despite the down times, managers often—though not always—feel excited, competent, and fulfilled in their jobs.

## "I'll learn the job primarily through training"

To increase your chances of succeeding in your new managerial role, you can prepare by taking advantage of any available management-training opportunities. Combined with talking with seasoned managers and starting out with realistic expectations, training can be a valuable tool.

But *in reality*, you can learn only so much through training. Your *best* teacher will be the on-the-job experience you accumulate as you begin actually serving in your new role. By taking on the right new experiences and learning from them, you can use your own insights to improve your performance and build your confidence.

To learn from your on-the-job experiences, you need to:

1. **Reflect on your on-the-job experiences.** Analyze what went right, what went wrong, and what you can do differently the next time you face a similar challenge.

2. **Gather feedback about your performance.** By getting input from peers, supervisors, direct reports, and other people on how you handled various challenges, you can better see the connections between your actions and their outcomes, and begin to match intent with impact. You can then hone your behaviors to achieve more of the results you want.

3. **Take time to identify and reflect on the key issues in situations you'll face.** By identifying key issues, you can figure out which lessons a new experience has to offer. For example, suppose you realize that your group must replace its customer-database system to help the company remain competitive. This kind of change initiative may raise the key issue of how to overcome employee resistance to learning a new system. If you anticipate this challenge ahead of time, you can watch for opportunities to learn how to address your employees' resistance as you begin implementing the change effort.

**Tip:** Identify the impact of your managerial style. Gather feedback from others not just on *what* you've done but also on *how* you've done it. This information helps you clarify cause-and-effect relationships and makes the link between your intentions and your actual impact on others.

# Understanding
# Complex
# Expectations

NEW MANAGERS MUST balance their own expectations of the role with those of their boss, peers, and employees. And sometimes these expectations can come into conflict. Below, we consider the complex expectations that arise when you become a manager.

## What you'll expect of yourself

When you become a manager, you enter the role with your own expectations of what your new job will involve. Often, those expectations differ from your job's *real* requirements. First-time leaders tend to focus on management's rights and privileges, not its duties and obligations. They expect to keep managing tasks (as they did before), not necessarily people—only with more power, control, and accountability than they had as individual contributors. They see their primary responsibilities as:

- Making task-related or operational decisions

- Hiring and firing direct reports

- Providing opportunities and innovative ideas

- Planning

But to accomplish these goals, managers will have to depend on other people—something many novice managers *don't* expect. Network- and relationship-building, along with "people challenges" such as conflict resolution and politicking, will constitute a major part of their job.

And because many new managers anticipate focusing on tasks rather than orchestrating their group's performance, they often cling to the "doer" role that they played so well as individual contributors.

## What your direct reports, bosses, and peers will expect of you

*Direct reports* see their manager's role in very different terms. In their view, a manager's job is to organize and direct the group's strategic goals; support direct reports as they accomplish tasks, including offering guidance, resources, and a sympathetic ear; and create the conditions that will help direct reports succeed—by providing leadership, keeping things running smoothly, anticipating long-term changes in the business environment, and building effective networks. Many direct reports also expect their boss to solve problems and answer questions decisively and represent their group to others inside and outside the organization.

Overall, direct reports have a relatively clear view of a manager's purpose: to get things done through others. At the same time, their viewpoint tends to be strongly influenced by their own interests: they expect their manager to serve their own needs and worries—first and foremost.

Meanwhile, in many *supervisors'* opinions, managers' responsibilities are primarily to accept final accountability for their unit, motivate direct reports to support corporate goals, and make trade-offs and manage risks. In supervisors' eyes, additional

# What Would YOU Do?

## "Am I *Really* Cut Out for This?"

AMILLA WAS FIVE HOURS into the worst day of work she had ever had. Just a few weeks ago, she had been promoted to manager of the company's sales force. Her pride and enthusiasm quickly faded as the pressures of her new position became apparent. Victor, one of her top salespeople, had left to take a job at another company. She couldn't understand it; Victor had been with the company for quite a few years. What had she done to make him leave? And then there was Ken, the head of the company's production department. Although Ken was a nice person and a good manager, Camilla was having trouble working with him. Ken was always making recommendations, from a production perspective, about how sales should conduct its business. Camilla appreciated his input, but had trouble balancing it with her own supervisors' expectations. She knew that she couldn't disappoint her supervisors just to maintain good relations with the production department. At the same time, she knew that without good relations with the production department, her team would not be able to do its job.

Camilla wanted to quit being a manager and go back to being liked by everyone else. She felt worn out by the pressure and the lack of sleep. She began to wonder whether she was really cut out for this job in the first place.

What would YOU do? The mentor will suggest a solution in *What You COULD Do.*

responsibilities include formulating and following well-thought-out plans, balancing the group's interests with those of others, and protecting the reputations of their superiors and the company.

In sum, supervisors tend to hold the most comprehensive and accurate view of what being a manager really entails. They emphasize managerial duties over rights and privileges, and people management over task management.

Finally, *peers*—managers in other functional areas—expect a new manager to represent his or her group or department; span boundaries between groups by sharing needed information and resources; set agendas and build networks, treat peers as partners, and do what's best for the company. Yet many new managers start off paying little attention to their peers' needs and expectations—usually because they feel overwhelmed by their new duties. However, they soon learn that their colleagues are counting on them to cultivate peer relationships as well as bonds with direct reports and supervisors.

---

Tip: Recognize interdependencies. Be aware of *mutual* dependencies—not just what you need from others or what others need from you. Use your power and influence to accomplish ends that are not entirely self-serving.

---

## How to manage conflicting expectations

When you become a manager, everyone you work with—from your supervisor to your peers to your direct reports—will have different expectations of you. Often, their expectations will conflict. How can you reconcile conflicting expectations? Hard-earned experience helps. Over time, you'll likely adopt more realistic expectations as you encounter the real limits to your power and control and interact with superiors, direct reports, and peers—including receiving requests, complaints, and feedback from all three groups. Grappling with inevitable conflicts and dilemmas and gaining experience with clearing the air of misunderstandings by communicating with those involved will also give you valuable practice in managing conflicting expectations.

Because direct reports have the closest physical presence, managers tend to be more responsive to their expectations. Next, because of the power relationship, new managers usually resolve conflicting views with their supervisors. Finally, new managers pay attention to their peers. However, all three groups are important and need your attention to start building productive relationships.

# What You COULD Do.

**Remember Camilla's worry that she may not be cut out for managerial work?**

Here's what the mentor suggests:

Becoming a manager is a big transition. It carries with it new roles and responsibilities—and seeing your organization with new perspectives. Camilla should remind herself that many new managers go through a period of uncertainty in regard to their new responsibilities. She should take the time to listen to and analyze what each constituency expects or wants and needs; she should not assume she knows it. It takes time to build credibility. But with time and practice, new managers gain the skills and confidence they need to excel in their new roles. Eventually, Camilla will learn how to transition from being an individual contributor to a new manager, manage the dynamics behind power and influence, and build effective, well-functioning teams—all essential responsibilities for the managerial role.

# Defining Your
# New Role

I N YOUR NEW ROLE as manager, you'll need to master the art of setting an agenda, building networks, and taking a broader view of your work. The sections below examine each of these in turn.

## Becoming an agenda setter

Setting an agenda for your group involves articulating strategies that will help your group support the company's objectives—and then ensuring that those strategies are implemented. To think like an agenda setter, you need to:

- View yourself as an entrepreneur who is running his or her own business—and who therefore must attend to all the forces that may make or break that business

- Broaden your perspective to include not just your group, but also the larger organization, as well as the industry and business environment in which your company operates

- Develop and maintain a budget to support your agenda

- Adopt a long-term orientation by thinking about various future scenarios and deciding how your group should respond

- Balance any tensions between your team or department and other groups in the organization, including clarifying priorities and making mutually acceptable compromises

- Accept that the priorities you identify may not necessarily be shared by your direct reports unless you communicate your vision to them

## Becoming a network builder

Building networks involves strengthening and sustaining mutually beneficial relationships with everyone you interact with—superiors, peers, and direct reports, as well as customers, suppliers, and people from partnering companies.

To think like a network builder, you need to:

- View yourself as a "people developer," not a "task doer"

- See the value in organizational politics as sharing and forming alliances

- Understand where you fit in the organization and how to use your position and personal qualities to achieve your goals and obtain needed resources—as well as help others do the same

- Grasp the importance of developing relationships with people outside as well as inside your group

- Be open to creating opportunities to spend time with bosses and peers—such as informal chats, lunches, meetings, and social interactions

- Be willing to participate actively in your organization and the larger community to build up the reputation of your group and company

Building networks—connections with other people—is easier for some than for others. But remember that practice makes this process familiar, and it's the only way to deal productively with the political realities of the business world.

## Taking a broader view

When you make the transition from individual contributor to manager, you not only revise your expectations and see yourself in a different light; you also begin viewing and handling problems and measuring success in whole new ways.

The problems you encountered as an individual contributor likely related directly to the particular tasks required in your job. Thus, each problem likely had one clear solution. However, most problems you'll face as a manager will have more than one solution. Try to envision or solicit as many solutions as possible. Also, define problems in broader, more holistic ways; in other words, view them as relevant to your entire group and organization, not just your own job. Finally, reconsider how you define success. As an individual contributor, you likely defined success in terms of your own performance—how many new customers you acquired, how well a new product you designed worked, and so forth. As a manager, however—someone whose primary responsibility is to get things done through others—you need to measure success differently. Specifically, your success will be defined by how well your *group* achieves its objectives, how much you've helped your direct reports hone their skills and manage tasks effectively, and how strongly your group's achievements have supported the company's objectives and strategies.

Just as success needs to be measured in new ways for a manager, satisfaction can take a different form. In the past, you may have been pleased with your own individual accomplishments, but now you need to *find satisfaction from different sources.* For one thing, you may be many steps removed from the outcome of your decisions and actions. As a result, your relationship to the outcome may be distant, ambiguous, or even unrecognized. You will rarely get the same instant gratification you got in the past with a successful outcome that was clearly your doing.

How can you still feel gratification under these changed conditions? Many managers learn to enjoy seeing and helping other people succeed. They discover that they can be effective coaches who bring out the best in others. They gradually adapt to their new identity and master their new responsibilities. They therefore get more of the results they want, and they make a larger impact on the company.

# Managing
# Teams

A TEAM IS MORE than just a group of individuals who work together. Rather, it's a small number of individuals with complementary skills who are committed to a common purpose, shared performance goals, and an approach to their mission for which they hold themselves collectively accountable. In this section, we'll explore the benefits of teamwork and ways to manage teams effectively.

## Why create teams?

For many business tasks or projects, a cohesive team can produce results that a set of individuals working solo could not. Teams are especially valuable when the work of your group or department:

- Requires a range or variety of knowledge, expertise, and perspective that can't be found in a single individual
- Involves interdependent tasks across individuals
- Calls for ownership and commitment on the part of all group members

When teams work well, the results can prove very productive. They may include increased performance and creativity, improved communication, more cross-training and development, and effective implementation of strategies and plans. Many of these advantages flow from the synergy of team members' skills and experiences. In addition, teams tend to establish new communication processes that encourage ongoing problem solving. Finally, many people enjoy, and are motivated by, working in teams. As a result, they deliver their best performance in a team setting.

## How to manage a team

Adapting your managerial style to fit a team situation doesn't have to mean "tacking on" a whole new approach that will feel unnatural, artificial, or phony to you. Rather, it's more like fine-tuning behaviors you're already doing, and weaving in some new behaviors that will help you better lead your team.

Consider the continua shown in the figure, "Four team-leadership continua," along which managers must be prepared to move as necessary.

**Four team-leadership continua**

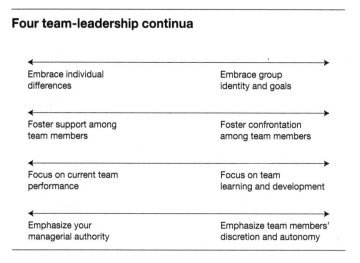

| | |
|---|---|
| Embrace individual differences | Embrace group identity and goals |
| Foster support among team members | Foster confrontation among team members |
| Focus on current team performance | Focus on team learning and development |
| Emphasize your managerial authority | Emphasize team members' discretion and autonomy |

Each of these continua illustrates a pair of conflicting forces, or tensions, that lie at the heart of team life. And, for each criterion, sometimes it's appropriate to gravitate toward one or the other polar end. Other times, it's appropriate to settle somewhere in the middle. It all depends on the needs of your team.

# Managing
# Individual
# Employees

**M**ANAGING INDIVIDUAL EMPLOYEES raises some unique challenges for a new manager. In this section, we take a closer look at strategies for getting the most from your individual direct reports.

## Understanding managerial styles

Just as it's important to adjust your team-management style, you need to adapt the way you lead different individuals within your group. That is, you need to provide different kinds of leadership for each individual, depending on, for example, his or her level of professional development or commitment to the job. The table "Adapting your managerial style" provides some examples.

For example, if you are a regional sales manager with a team of salespeople, you need to assess what each team member needs from you—and those needs will be very different!

- A new hire will take more of your time, requiring careful instructions and guidance. You will need to observe him often as he tackles the new skills, giving him suggestions, feedback, and guidance. If, however, you let this person go on his own, he will likely make many mistakes, and feel abandoned and discouraged.

- On the other hand, the top salesperson who has been on the job for fifteen years needs little guidance. Just give this person all the room she needs to carry on and do the best job possible. You might even ask her to be a mentor for the new hire. If you misjudge what she needs and manage her too closely, as though she were a new hire, she will become frustrated, even angry about your lack of trust in her.

Individuals need different *degrees* and *kinds* of professional development and commitment. Therefore, you apply different

## Adapting your managerial style

| Developmental/ commitment level | Example | Appropriate managerial style |
|---|---|---|
| Beginner | A team member is just starting out in his or her career, or is taking on a new position or task. | **Directive** Monitor the person more closely, and provide more explicit instructions and demands. |
| Disillusioned | A team member feels bitter or resentful about problems in the team. | **Coaching** Identify the person's concerns, and work together with him or her to move past them. |
| Reluctant | A team member lacks confidence to fully engage in the work at hand. | **Supportive** Encourage the person to identify his or her strengths and build on them, and to gradually take more risks. |
| Peak performance | A team member is at the top of his or her "game." | **Delegating** Give the person significant latitude, and entrust him or her with key task responsibilities and decision making. |

*degrees* and *kinds* of direction, coaching, support, and delegation as appropriate.

## Knowing when and how to give feedback

In business, feedback is the sharing of observations about job performance or work-related behaviors for the purpose of reinforcing effective behaviors and changing ineffective ones. Although similar to coaching in some ways, feedback is a more direct form of intervention and can occur with or without the recipient's consent.

By giving feedback, you aim to be helpful and constructive, *not* critical and judgmental. Your goal is to offer advice on ways to improve, *not* to enumerate another person's faults. Depending on your needs, you can give feedback to someone based on that person's short-term or long-term goals. You can also give feedback in different directions: upward to your boss, downward to a direct report, or laterally to a colleague or peer.

As a new manager, you may want to *give* feedback to help a direct report, your boss, or a peer achieve his or her work objectives. You may also want to *elicit* feedback from your direct reports, boss, or peers to improve your own performance. Regardless of who the recipient is, effective feedback can help these aspects of his or her work:

- **Relationships**—how well the person interacts with others

- **Process**—how the individual gets his or her work done

- **Results**—how the person performs on measurable, on-the-job achievements

# Using coaching

Coaching is a partnership between two people—usually a manager and a direct report—in which both parties share knowledge and experience in order to maximize the coachee's potential and help him or her achieve agreed-upon goals. It is a shared act in which the coachee actively and willingly participates. The table "What is coaching?" provides more details about what coaching is and is not.

You and a direct report may agree to form a coaching relationship when both of you believe that working together will lead to

## What is coaching?

| Coaching is . . . | Coaching is not . . . |
|---|---|
| A means for learning and development | A time to criticize |
| A way to guide someone toward his or her goals | A means for directing someone's actions in order to meet your own goals |
| The sharing of experiences and opinions to generate agreed-upon outcomes | A chance to be the expert or supervisor with "all the answers" |
| A means for inspiring and supporting another person | A way to address personal issues |

*Source:* Adapted from Interaction Associates

improved performance. Through coaching, you can help direct reports to:

- Maximize their strengths (for example, build on analytical skills)

- Overcome personal obstacles (for instance, reduce a fear of public speaking)

- Achieve new skills and competencies (for example, develop more advanced communication skills)

- Prepare themselves for new responsibilities (such as leading a special project)

- Manage themselves (for instance, find ways to improve their use of time)

- Clarify and work toward performance goals (for example, learn to set more realistic goals)

## Understanding the "triangle of relationships"

One way to think about managing teams and individuals is to imagine a triangle made up of three sets of relationships:

- Your relationship to your team as a whole

- Your relationship to each of your team's members as individuals

- Individual members' relationship to the team as a whole

Relationships along one "leg" of the triangle affect relationships along the other two legs. If you overemphasize one set of relationships at the expense of the other two, your team's performance can suffer. For example, if you pay *too* much attention to your role as manager of the whole team, some team members may complain that you're not acknowledging their individual contributions. They then begin withholding their best thinking from the team, because they feel that their contributions won't be noticed. Over time, the team as a whole becomes passive and uninvolved. You decide that the team is "ungrateful," and withdraw your support. Tension mounts, and overall team performance declines.

Moderation often seems to be a key to success. The more you can balance the three sets of relationships, the healthier, happier, and more productive your team will likely be.

# Promoting Diversity
# and Group Culture

I N ADDITION TO LEARNING how to manage teams and individuals, you'll need to master the art of leveraging diversity in your group as well as shaping its culture. Let's consider each of these in turn.

## Understanding forms of diversity

For many people, the word *diversity* has come to connote primarily racial/ethnic, demographic, or gender differences among employees within a company. And certainly such differences can influence the assumptions that people make about each other and the way they work together. But diversity can occur on many other dimensions, some "visible" and some "invisible." Your supervisors, peers, and direct reports can differ in many ways:

- **Experience.** Some individuals may be just out of college and entering the workforce for the first time; others may be quite experienced.

- **Cultural background.** People may come from different regions of the country or from other countries entirely.

- **Physical ability.** Some people may use various forms of assistive technologies, such as voice-activated software, to perform their work.

- **Working or learning style.** Some people approach a task logically and methodically; others are more intuitive and creative.

All these differences can strongly influence people's needs, ways of communicating and interacting, and priorities.

## Grasping intangible dimensions of diversity

People also differ along some more abstract (but deeply personal) dimensions. These differences can make building relationships with direct reports especially challenging. For instance, your direct reports may have markedly different:

- **Professional motivations.** Some people may be aiming for a career in management themselves; others may wish to continue serving as individual contributors. And some employees may be far more or less driven than others to perform at their best.

- **Management preferences.** Some people may want more direction from you than others do. And some may want more or less contact with you (in the form of regular meetings or e-mail exchanges).

- **Personal style.** Each subordinate will have his or her own way of interacting with others, dealing with conflict, and so forth. Unfortunately, some direct reports may prove problematic; for example, they have little motivation to work, or they have an overbearing or otherwise troublesome personality trait that alienates or distracts their fellow team members.

Taken together, all these differences create both the challenges and the richness that you can expect to encounter when you first become a manager. The deep differences between people can lead to misunderstandings or other difficulties, but they can also serve as the very sources of the special contributions that each person brings to your team.

Indeed, the more diverse your team is, the greater the variety of ideas, perspectives, solutions to problems, skills, and personal abilities your group has to offer. These are resources you will need to learn to leverage.

## Understanding group culture

When you step into your new role as manager of an existing group, you may discover something surprising: the team you'll be leading already has its own culture—that is, a distinct way of solving problems, getting work done, communicating, learning, dealing with conflict, interacting with other groups, and marking successes and dealing with disappointments. Your group's culture may have been shaped by its former leader's personal style and expectations, the styles and expectations of the group members, and the particular life stages and challenges the group has experienced.

A key step in building effective relationships with your new direct reports is avoiding trying to make improvements too soon. First, spend time learning about the culture you've inherited. Only then can you determine how best to help team members succeed individually and collectively in progressing toward your strategic goals.

## Shaping the culture of a new group

New managers often make the following assumptions when faced with an inherited group:

- All their direct reports are similar to one another in terms of their work and personal styles, cultural backgrounds, and so forth.

- All group members have the same motivations, goals, and values that they, the managers, have.

- Leaders must treat all their employees the same in order to treat them fairly.

Even when differences among individuals in the group become apparent, some managers assume that they can mold employees in their own image—that is, change them so that they resemble the managers themselves. But this effort commonly results in resistance and resentment from employees.

First, acknowledge that each member of your group is a unique person with individual personalities, skills, and attitudes. Then take the following action steps.

1. **Get to know your direct reports.** Find out by talking, asking, and observing the answers to questions such as "How do team members prefer to be managed?" "What motivates them

(logic? emotional appeal? exciting new ideas?)?" "Who needs a firm hand?" "Who needs a lot of praise?" "How do they respond to conflict?"

2. **Decide how best to treat each employee *fairly* to help him or her succeed.** To some managers, fair treatment means identical treatment. But fairness really means finding the best ways to help *each* direct report succeed. And those ways may differ, depending on your direct reports' different situations. Thus, when you treat people differently, you're actually giving them an *equal opportunity* to do well.

For example, suppose you're about to become the manager of a product-development group. In what ways could you help each member of the group fairly? One person responds to praise with renewed energy, commitment, and creativity. You make it a point to thank him in person at least once a week for whatever recent successes he has achieved. Another group member is highly motivated by the idea that the products your group develops can help make consumers' lives better. In discussing new product ideas, you take time to mention to her how a particular new device might make people's lives healthier, more enjoyable or convenient, or better in some other specific, important way. Finally, yet another individual has a tendency to suffer repetitive-motion injuries if he spends too much time working at a computer. You research and invest in a voice-activated software product that will let him excel at his job without risking injury.

# Embracing Your New Identity

MANY FIRST-TIME leaders are aware that they'll need to master new management skills and competencies in order to succeed in their new role. However, they may not realize that the managerial role will change who they are as *persons*. As you begin devoting yourself to your new job, you'll experience shifts along these three dimensions:

- Your motivations for being a manager

- Your assessment of your ability to do the job

- Your professional identity

Let's examine each of these in turn.

## Understanding your motivations

Many soon-to-be managers look forward to their new role because they believe it will let them assume more authority and responsibility, make more money, exercise more power and influence, and improve inefficient practices and show others the right way to do things. They may also believe that they'll achieve new prestige and status, gain recognition for contributing to their organization's success, and use the managerial role as a stepping-stone for even higher positions in the company.

Any or all of these objectives may be relevant, important, and achievable for some managers. But soon after taking on their new responsibilities, newly minted managers discover something surprising: their job is not so much about them, their power, and their success—it's about their group and *its* effectiveness and success. Indeed, as we've seen, first-time managers are often dismayed to find that they have far less power and prestige than they expected, the criteria for measuring their performance are less clear than when they were individual contributors, and seeing their efforts bear fruit can take a long time.

On the other hand, becoming an effective manager lets you help your people to excel and fulfill their own dreams. You also see your employees gain new skills and self-confidence, and open new salary and career opportunities for members of your group. And finally, you come to recognize that the scale and scope of your impact on the organization can be much larger when you are a manager rather than an individual contributor.

Whatever your original motivations for wanting to become a manager, be honest with yourself and be open to change!

## Assessing your ability to do the job

As you step into the managerial role, your questions may shift from "Will I like being a manager?" to "Will I be good at it?" To gauge your impact as a manager:

- **Assess your influence on specific individuals, especially direct reports.** For example, a sales manager coaches a sales rep on how to close deals, and then watches to see whether the rep increases the number of closed deals that quarter.

- **Notice how you might be affecting the group culture.** For instance, a manager who has a natural ability to use humor to inspire others begins noticing that her direct reports are now using humor to boost morale among themselves.

- **Ask others about your impact on the organization.** Gather varied impressions about your style, work, or influence from different sources—including direct reports, peers, bosses, and customers. To illustrate, request that your supervisor conduct a three-month performance review for you.

- **Develop your own objective criteria to evaluate your performance.** For example, track the turnover rate in your group, the number and quality of customer complaints, and so forth.

- **Look for common or contrasting patterns in the feedback you receive.** For instance, you may discover that direct reports as well as your supervisor see you as somewhat timid, while others see you as overly aggressive.

- **Pay attention to your own behavior, analyzing how you handle various situations.** To illustrate, observe how you greet direct reports at the beginning of the workday. Do you smile and say hello to each group member? Or do you dash into your office and start your day by checking e-mail and phone messages instead?

- **Begin to develop a set of peer coaches.** Find people you can turn to for help or to broaden your point of view.

By collecting different kinds of information from various sources, you can assemble evidence in the same way you'd put together a jigsaw puzzle. The resulting impressions will give you a full picture of your impact on the company.

## Recognizing the new you

As you accumulate experience in your new role, you'll discover whole new sides of yourself. Some of these discoveries may be encouraging. For example, perhaps you find that many of your colleagues and direct reports see you as more empathetic and supportive than you see yourself. Or maybe you learn that you have unexpected reserves of enthusiasm and fresh perspectives, or that you're especially talented at giving people constructive feedback on both their good points and their areas for improvement.

But other discoveries may be disturbing. For instance, maybe you realize that others see you as too aggressive, demanding, self-interested, dictatorial, harsh, indecisive, or some other undesirable quality. Or perhaps you have less self-confidence than you thought.

Remember: *you* are directing your own identity shift. You need to reconcile your intent with your impact. How do you want to be perceived by others, and what is the actual impact of your behavior on others? Your task is to acknowledge conflicting views and realities and take steps to address them.

# Strengthening Your Emotional Intelligence

U NDERSTANDING YOURSELF and others can help you weather and direct the personal shifts you'll experience as a new manager. But how can you actually deepen your knowledge of your own and others' motivations, strengths, and weaknesses? One way is through strengthening and using your *emotional intelligence*—a combination of self-management skills and the ability to work with others.

## What is emotional intelligence?

Emotional intelligence (EI) comprises five components, as shown in the table "Components of emotional intelligence."

**Components of emotional intelligence**

SELF-MANAGEMENT SKILLS

| Skill | Definition | Example |
|-------|-----------|---------|
| **1. Self-awareness** | Knowing and being willing to talk about your weaknesses | You work poorly under tight deadlines, so you plan your time carefully—and explain to colleagues why you're careful about your schedule. |

| Skill | Definition | Example |
|---|---|---|
| **2. Self-regulation** | Having the ability to control your impulses and channel them for good purposes | Your group stumbles during an important presentation. Instead of kicking over a chair or glaring angrily at everyone, you take time to assess the situation. You acknowledge the failure, consider possible reasons for it, and then call your team together, offer your feelings, and work together to learn from the mistakes. |
| **3. Motivation** | Being motivated by an internal drive to achieve, not by external rewards | You seek out creative challenges, love to learn, and take great pride in a job well done. You also constantly explore new and better approaches to your work. |

**ABILITY TO RELATE TO OTHERS**

| Skill | Definition | Example |
|---|---|---|
| **4. Empathy** | Taking others' feelings into account when making decisions | You assign one direct report to a prized project, leaving others disappointed. You take the feelings of the unhappy ones into account and find ways to treat everyone fairly in the long run. |
| **5. Social skill** | Building rapport with others, inspiring them to cooperate, and moving them in the direction you desire | You're convinced that your company's future lies with the Internet. You find like-minded people and use your social skill to stitch together a virtual community of support cutting across levels, functions, and divisions. You use this de facto team to create a prototype of an innovative corporate Web site, and you recruit people from various company units to represent your firm at an important Internet industry convention. |

## Enhancing your EI

To strengthen your emotional intelligence:

- Gather feedback from colleagues to shed light on which of your EI skills most need improvement.

- Practice new EI behaviors as often as possible; for example, remind yourself to express anger or frustration in new, more productive ways than you have in the past (such as taking a brisk walk).

- Make a personal commitment to developing your EI.

Like other forms of professional development, enhancing your EI takes effort, time, and patience. However, the investment will pay big dividends. One global food and beverage company discovered this firsthand—when managers who worked to develop their EI outperformed their own yearly earnings goals by 20 percent.

# Coping with
# New Feelings

A S YOU'RE EMBARKING on your new role as a manager, how are you feeling? Most new managers feel excited, proud, and anxious, even fearful of their changing role. And if you're like many businesspeople in general, you may feel reluctant to acknowledge or talk about these emotions. After all, the workplace should be ruled by logic and rationality—not feelings—right?

But if you understand that your feelings are perfectly normal, you'll be less likely to be surprised by them. You can also prepare yourself to better manage the emotional challenges and strains that accompany the transition into management.

## What to expect

You can expect to experience one or more of the following emotions as you transition from individual contributor to manager:

- **Frustration**—especially if you suspect that your responses to new demands just aren't working

- **Performance anxiety**—or the fear of failure

- **Loss**—as you bid farewell to your familiar identity, your sense of mastery, and all the other satisfying things you had as an individual contributor

- **Humility**—as you discover that you may not be as prepared for your new role as you thought

- **Marginality**—a sense of being caught between two identities

Typically, new managers have the *least* tolerance for performance anxiety, or fear of failure. Why? Many managers have a long history as high achievers in their individual-contributor role. So they find it especially difficult to imagine coping with the feelings of shame and guilt that they know often accompany failure. In addition, they typically lack the experience and skills to deal with those unfamiliar emotions.

The first step to dealing with these emotions is to realize that they are normal. The second is to realize that they will naturally diminish over time as you gain the skills and confidence you need to excel in your new position. And the third is to take action to relieve the stress associated with these emotions. To relieve stress, start by understanding the causes behind the emotional turmoil that many novice managers experience. We'll look at these causes below.

## Role strain

Role strain derives from the overload, ambiguity, and conflict woven into the managerial role. Managers discover that they have *too much* work to do—in the face of insufficient time and information, and limited resources; they have *conflicting responsibilities*, such as increasing revenues while also holding down costs; and they have to *answer to too many people*—superiors, customers,

# What Would YOU Do?

### The Case of the Talented but Troublesome Trader

S UZANNE WAS RECENTLY promoted to "head trader" of the high-tech global securities trading desk at DrayCo, an investment services firm. She knew the transition from trader to *manager* of traders would be challenging, but she never expected it to be this difficult. She has done a good job of learning how to build relationships with her traders so as to gain their support for new initiatives she wants to propose. For example, she chats frequently in the hallway with them, suggests they grab a bite to eat for lunch, and asks them for advice.

However, Suzanne is having trouble managing one of her direct reports. Chen, the most senior trader in her group, complains frequently about problems within the team and sometimes ignores Suzanne's requests. At times, he doesn't engage fully in the work at hand. Despite his negative demeanor, Chen is a highly talented trader. Suzanne wants to keep him in the group, but she doesn't want Chen's attitude to corrode the team's morale. Yet she's not sure how to begin addressing this challenge.

What would YOU do? The mentor will suggest a solution in *What You COULD Do*.

direct reports, peers—all of whom make managers feel pulled in multiple directions.

Role strain also stems from other characteristics of the managerial position, such as the fast pace and constant interruptions, the fact that managers can't neatly plan and control every moment of their day and that their decisions require compromises among competing interests, and managers' own lack of knowledge—since they can't be experts on the many issues they confront each day.

## Endless problem solving

Endless problem solving is another source of stress. Direct reports tend to bring their most knotty problems and frustrations to their manager—and expect him or her to solve them. New managers may feel overwhelmed by direct reports' relentless focus on problems and the department's or group's shortcomings, and become discouraged because most of these problems don't have simple solutions.

In addition, managers may discover that some of their direct reports may not be as motivated or competent as they themselves had been as individual contributors. Indeed, dealing with "problem employees" can constitute a unique source of negativity.

New managers eventually find it easier to endure these frustrating aspects of management. They learn to draw boundaries around what kinds of problems they'll take on, and they resist the urge to classify all direct reports who come to them with concerns as problem employees.

## Isolation

Most managers are social beings. They enjoy interacting with others and had plenty of human contact as individual contributors. By contrast, the managerial role can be lonely at times. That's because:

- New supervisors don't yet "know the ropes"—the wisdom about their jobs that will come only with experience.

- At times, managers must make decisions that are unpopular with direct reports. As a result, they sense mistrust, resentment, and rejection from their subordinates.

- Direct reports who used to be a manager's peers now seem to avoid casual social contact with him or her.

To overcome a sense of isolation, seek support and companionship from other individuals—friends and past coworkers—in the larger organization. Many new managers feel reluctant to call on these relationships early in their tenure, because they fear that these people will see them as weak or incompetent. However, these individuals can provide invaluable support—just when you need it most.

## Burdens of leadership

Having so much authority and responsibility can be disconcerting for a new manager. And leadership does present three burdens that can prove particularly stressful for inexperienced managers:

- **Managing risk.** The stakes are higher for a manager than for an individual contributor. Managers must make important decisions under imperfect conditions. This requires them to build confidence, a strong will, and the ability to feel comfortable exercising power and influence—while accepting and learning from an occasional bad decision.

In honestly admitting their mistakes, imperfect decisions, and limitations, many leaders are surprised to discover that their power is not at all diminished. Indeed, their honesty helps direct reports see them as real human beings—and thus more approachable and credible.

- **Being a role model.** Numerous first-time managers soon realize that their actions have lasting consequences for the people around them. In particular, they learn that they need to manage their emotions—appearing enthusiastic and optimistic, and conveying a sense of maturity and professionalism.

  They also find that their direct reports look to them for cues on how to behave, particularly during times of stress. Thus, managers need to learn how to appear calm during difficult times.

- **Having power over other people's lives.** In influencing others' work and lives, managers face two particularly difficult challenges: (1) taking disciplinary action, such as firing an employee, and (2) balancing individual and group interests.

  Firing someone can be enormously unsettling and sobering—especially when a manager cares about the person and knows the impact the loss of the job will have on him or her. Many managers take a direct report's failure—or, for that matter, an employee's voluntary decision to move to another company—as a personal failure.

As a manager, you do need to examine your own role in a direct report's failure to perform, because you may have been part of the problem. If so, find ways to avoid such problematic behavior in the future.

## Easing the strain

In light of the many stresses and emotions associated with both the transition to the managerial role and the pressures inherent in the job, what can you, a new manager, do to keep from burning yourself out? One helpful step is to know ahead of time what stresses and emotions to expect. Another is to take action to relieve the stress. Here are some additional ideas:

- **Don't neglect your personal life.** Cutting yourself off from your family and friends can only worsen your feelings of isolation. Indeed, many managers find that a spouse, a relationship partner, a respected relative, or a close friend can provide enormous emotional support during this challenging career transition.

- **Get enough leisure time and relaxation.** If necessary, force yourself to periodically take a day—or even a half day—off. During your time off, try not to think about work. Instead, engage in whatever activities you find most rejuvenating—such as reading a novel, taking a long walk, or playing your favorite sport.

- **Talk about your concerns with supportive friends.** People both inside and outside your organization with whom you have close friendships can provide crucial emotional support. Talk with them about what you're going through. Even if they do nothing but listen, you'll almost certainly feel better after getting your concerns out in the open.

- **Take care of your health.** If you're experiencing physical problems as a result of job stress, take advantage of every opportunity to relax. If you're used to exercising regularly, carve out time to stick to your regimen. Many people find that even just a twenty-minute walk or jog can clear their heads and rejuvenate their energy. Perhaps most important, try to get enough sleep. Fatigue is notorious for making even the most minor problem look far worse than it really is.

- **Keep your job in proper perspective.** When your managerial role seems about to overwhelm you, take a moment to reappraise your values and personal and professional commitments. Ask yourself, "What's *most* important to me? What *really* counts in life?" And remember: no job or career—no matter how exciting, stimulating, or financially rewarding—is worth your sanity, your physical health, or your commitments to family or friends.

All of the above tips can help ease the strain of serving as a manager. But perhaps the most important advice to keep in mind is, *be patient with yourself.* Know that, in time, your ability to cope with the pressures of management will improve. As you gain familiarity with your job and all its inherent stresses, you'll uncover internal resources you never knew you had.

# What You COULD Do.

**Remember Suzanne's concern over how to handle Chen's negative behavior?**

Here's what the mentor suggests:

Since Chen appears dissatisfied and disengaged, Suzanne should get to the root of his disengagement problem to help him move past his concerns.

In this situation, she should use a coaching leadership style. Coaching—a process by which a manager helps a direct report identify and move past problem behaviors—is the best leadership approach in this case.

Part of being a good manager is adapting the way you lead your team and the individuals within it. Suzanne needs to fine-tune her approach to each person on her team—depending on each individual's level of professional development and commitment to the job.

# Reaping the Rewards of Being a Manager

E VENTUALLY, THE HARD work of transitioning into the managerial role will pay dividends. You'll find that you're satisfying important psychological needs, developing your professional skills, and collaborating more than ever with others. Enjoy these rewards—you've worked hard to earn them!

## Satisfying important psychological needs

Becoming an effective manager enables you to satisfy some important psychological needs:

- **Achievement.** You already know you have a need for achievement. Otherwise, you probably would not have excelled as an individual contributor. Nor would you have been likely to take on the difficult job of manager. But the role of manager gives you the opportunity to achieve in new ways. Specifically, you learn about and master new skills, accomplish important work in challenging new ways, and support your company's vision and mission in new ways.

- **Influence.** Being a manager is all about exercising influence. In the workplace, influencing others to achieve shared goals can be very satisfying. As a manager, you develop networks of relationships with the many different people on whom you depend to get things done. Over time, you get to know what's most important to each of these individuals, how you can best help them achieve their goals, and how they can best help you. You exchange information and other resources in mutually supportive, beneficial ways.

- **Affiliation.** Many managers have a need for affiliation—being part of and contributing to something larger than just themselves. Our connections with other people can deeply satisfy our need for affiliation, and our jobs often help us satisfy this deep need. The managerial role provides numerous opportunities to collaborate with others to accomplish shared goals that transcend your personal aims.

## Developing and growing

As you encounter entirely new kinds of challenges and responsibilities in the managerial role, you find that you have the strength and resources to meet these challenges. For example, perhaps you'll ultimately learn that you have a gift for leading and inspiring others. Or you'll find that you're especially talented at gauging others' motivations and values.

Each time you make something happen as a manager—whether it's shaping your group's culture in positive ways, helping someone master a new task, or assembling a top-notch team—you expand your abilities. You become a more seasoned, experienced, and confident leader, and you have a sharper awareness of your own strengths and areas for improvement.

Not only do you learn more about yourself as you progress in your role; you also learn more about organizational life in general, including how influence really works, what makes one team more effective than another, and how your own group's strategies and activities can support (or hinder) the larger organization's goals.

## Collaborating

In the workplace, good ideas have the *most* impact when people work together to turn them into products or services that satisfy customers' needs and support the organization's mission. As a manager, you play a central role in that collaborative process by:

- Developing a top-notch team

- Using your influence to cultivate commitment and a cooperative spirit among your peers, your own supervisors, your direct reports, and key players *outside* your company, such as suppliers, customers, and partnering organizations

- Winning your direct reports' loyalty

- Helping others succeed

## Tips for Leveraging Resources in Your First Year

- Know your major resources. Remember, you've got three major resources at your disposal: (1) your previous career experiences, (2) the people you already know, and (3) your formal training.
- Use previous supervisors as models. Think about the people who supervised you. What were their strengths and weaknesses?

Which of their attributes could you emulate to develop your own management and decision-making skills?

- Use previous supervisors as advisers. If possible, stay in touch with these individuals, and ask them for advice.
- Ask your current supervisor to be your coach. If your current boss has a reputation as a skilled people developer, call on him or her for advice on your transition process.
- Stay in touch with previous and current peers. Meet with these individuals as often as possible to discuss your ideas, interpret your experiences, and spot connections between your actions and their outcomes.
- Use formal training opportunities to augment on-the-job learning. Take advantage of all formal training offered to you.

# Tips and Tools

# Tools for
# Becoming a New Manager

## *Best Manager–Worst Manager*

*Use this worksheet alone or with a group to evaluate the characteristics of the best and worst managers you've ever worked with. Thinking about what kind of a manager you want to be is a valuable task as you start out on the path of being a manager.*

| The Worst Manager I Ever Had | The Best Manager I Ever Had |
|---|---|
| List characteristics below, especially those that you want to avoid doing yourself. | List characteristics below, especially those that you would like to develop for yourself. |
| | |
| | |
| | |
| | |
| | |
| | |
| | |
| | |
| | |

**What I Learned from This Exercise**

*Use this space to record the important observations you've discovered in the exercise above. You may find it interesting to keep this list and periodically review it.*

# Checklist for New Managers

*Use this checklist to identify gaps between the skills you used in your prior position and those you will need in your new one. New skills will take time to learn and practice; think about which ones you need the most or need first.*

| Skill or Competency | Part of My Prior Position Responsibilities | Part of My New Manager Responsibilities |
|---|---|---|
| Supervising employees | | |
| Assessing performance | | |
| Setting goals | | |
| Delegating | | |
| Hiring | | |
| Coaching | | |
| Leading a team | | |
| Recruiting | | |
| Budgeting | | |
| Salary administration | | |
| Explaining and enforcing policies | | |
| Creating a vision; having a big-picture perspective | | |
| Managing for results; ensuring that goals are accomplished | | |
| Conducting layoffs if required | | |
| Dismissing an employee if required | | |
| Supporting others in the accomplishment of their goals | | |
| Managing the level of workplace activity and stress | | |
| Making presentations | | |
| Establishing alliances | | |
| Running meetings | | |
| Managing my time | | |
| Supporting developmental opportunities for staff | | |
| Providing direction | | |
| Adapting my style to meet others' needs if indicated | | |
| Motivating others | | |
| Providing leadership | | |
| Fostering innovation or creativity | | |
| Assigning job responsibilities | | |
| Managing projects | | |
| Balancing and setting priorities | | |
| Conducting disciplinary sessions | | |
| Interviewing | | |

## Emotional Intelligence Self-Assessment

*Use this tool to think about your emotional intelligence, or the ability to manage yourself and your relationships effectively.*

| Emotional Intelligence Capabilities | Rating | | |
|---|---|---|---|
| | Adequate | A Strength | Needs Improvement |
| **Self-Awareness** | | | |
| I am self-confident. | | | |
| I know my strengths and limitations. | | | |
| I know when to ask for help. | | | |
| **Self-Regulation** | | | |
| I am trustworthy. | | | |
| I am in control of my feelings and impulses. | | | |
| I suspend judgment and prefer to seek out information. | | | |
| **Motivation** | | | |
| I have a strong drive to achieve. | | | |
| I am optimistic even in the face of failure. | | | |
| I constantly try to improve. | | | |
| **Empathy** | | | |
| I have expertise in coaching and retaining talented people. | | | |
| I am sensitive to cross-cultural differences. | | | |
| I intuitively know how people are feeling. | | | |
| **Social Skills** | | | |
| I have expertise in building and leading teams. | | | |
| I have a knack for finding common ground with others. | | | |
| I enjoy collaboration. | | | |

# Contact Sheet for New Managers

*A critical task for managers is to know how and where they can get the information or assistance they need. This is more of a challenge for new managers in a new company. It takes time to develop real alliances, but a simple contact list such as the one below can help you get off to a good start. You can modify this list as new needs present themselves.*

| When I Need Information or Advice on ... | I'll Go to ... Person Responsible | Phone, E-mail, or Location |
|---|---|---|
| Security | | |
| Benefits, insurance, policies, and procedures | | |
| Technology, my desktop system | | |
| IT help desk or hot line | | |
| Purchasing, accounts payable, receivable, and so on | | |
| Training for myself or my direct reports | | |
| Records, departmental | | |
| Records, employee files | | |
| Physical plant maintenance | | |
| Performance management | | |
| Coaching | | |
| Salary levels and administration | | |
| Budgeting | | |
| Affirmative Action, Equal Employment Opportunity | | |
| Hiring or recruitment | | |
| Mailing, shipment | | |
| Warehouse, inventory levels | | |
| Mailing, express delivery | | |
| Organizational charts, structure | | |
| Temporary help agency | | |
| Sales | | |
| Marketing | | |
| Public relations, publicity | | |
| Engineering | | |
| Production | | |
| Legal advice | | |
| Customer service | | |
| Customer service number | | |
| Returns and refunds | | |

## *Adapting Your Managerial Style*

*Use this worksheet to think through how you might adapt your managerial style to complement the needs and developmental level of your direct reports. Who needs more direction? Support? Whom should you leave on their own as much as possible? There are numerous ways of thinking about how to adapt your style. The following is just one. Use the following guidelines to focus on each employee, his or her needs, and what style you could adopt that would help them perform the best and feel motivated and rewarded.*

**Developmental Levels of Employees**

| | |
|---|---|
| **Beginning level** | New to the job, perhaps new to the company. Needs direction, supervision, and support. May have low competence level due to inexperience. May be enthusiastic about this new opportunity. |
| **Moderate level** | Has developed competence but is not performing at peak levels yet. Needs coaching and support. May at times become disillusioned as the reality of the job and challenges sets in. |
| **High level** | A peak performer, most likely very experienced. Needs less direct supervision, and may resent it. Think about ways to delegate tasks and keep the person feeling challenged. |

| Direct Report | Developmental Commitment Level | Appropriate Managerial Style |
|---|---|---|
| *Example: Jane Doe* | *Beginner: Jane is just starting out in her career and is taking on new responsibilities.* | *Directive: You monitor the person more closely and provide more explicit instructions and demands.* |
| | | |
| | | |
| | | |
| | | |
| | | |

# Test Yourself

This section offers ten multiple-choice questions to help you identify your baseline knowledge of what's involved in becoming a manager. Answers to the questions are given at the end of the test.

**1.** Which of the following is not a common myth about management?

   a. Managers have a lot of power.

   b. Managers have a lot of inner strength.

   c. Managers have a lot of freedom.

**2.** Which of the following would suggest that you had succeeded as a manager?

   a. Your group has achieved its objective of boosting sales by a specific percentage this quarter.

   b. You've personally resolved most of the customer complaints coming through your department.

   c. You've completed a challenging management seminar and have stayed with the job for one year.

**3.** What is a manager's most important source of power?

   a. His or her formal authority.

   b. His or her professional and educational qualifications.

   c. His or her personal influence.

**4.** Which of the following expectation is the most likely to be fulfilled when you become a manager?

   a. You'll achieve new status, prestige, and recognition for contributing to your organization's success.

   b. You'll help your people to excel, fulfill their own dreams, and gain new skills and self-confidence.

   c. You'll be able to make decisions more quickly and therefore see the results of your actions right away.

**5.** What is the most productive method to manage a new team member?

   a. Work with the person closely and provide ongoing feedback and guidance.

   b. Let the person learn through his or her mistakes.

   c. Have the person read business guides, attend training sessions, and seek help in solving problems.

**6.** True or false: In order to treat your direct reports fairly, you must treat them all the same.

   a. True.

   b. False.

**7.** Which of the following best describes what a team is?

   a. A team is a group of people who work on a single, defined project together; disband or reorganize after the project is finished; and receive new assignments based on company needs.

   b. A team is a group of people who have a common purpose, shared performance goals, and an approach to their mission for which they hold themselves collectively accountable.

   c. A team is a group of people who place a higher priority on their learning and development versus their current performance, and who emphasize mutual support over confrontation.

**8.** What is coaching?

   a. A two-way partnership in which both parties share knowledge and experience in order to maximize the coachee's potential and help him or her achieve agreed-upon goals.

   b. A way for you to impart desired values, skills, and attitudes to an employee so that his or her performance or behavior will more strongly support your goals and agenda.

   c. A way for managers to help employees address personal issues that are making it difficult for them to contribute to the team's efforts or hone their own performance.

**9.** What's the best way you can combat the feeling of being over-whelmed when your team seems to constantly bring problems to you?

a. Let employees know that you support them—that you're committed to listening to and resolving their problems whenever they need your help.

b. Coach employees to strengthen their own problem-solving skills, and encourage them to come to you only with problems they can't solve on their own.

c. Have a frank group discussion about each team member's role. Explain that employees must take responsibility for resolving their own problems.

**10.** Being an effective manager provides opportunities to satisfy which of the following needs?

a. Your direct reports' approval and peers' respect.

b. Job security and a well-defined career path.

c. Achievement, influence, and affiliation.

## Answers to test questions

**1, b.** Some managers may indeed have a lot of inner strength—but most first-time leaders don't go into their new role saddled with incorrect assumptions about inner strength. Instead, they fall prey to myths about what kinds of skills managers need, how much power and freedom they have, how they feel about their jobs, and how valuable training might be in helping them master their new role.

**2, a.** At its core, management means getting things done through other people. Thus managers must measure their success by gauging how well their *group* achieves its objectives. But they must also attend to other factors—such as how much they've helped their direct reports hone their skills and how strongly their group's achievements have supported the company's objectives and strategies. These measures differ markedly from those used to gauge individual contributors' success.

**3, c.** Personal influence is a far greater source of power than a person's formal authority or professional and education qualifications. That's because direct reports don't simply follow their manager's direction, unless they see you as credible. And credibility takes time to cultivate. Moreover, managers don't have any formal authority over their peers and supervisors—two groups whose support they still need to get things done. Rather than relying on formal authority or professional and educational qualifications, managers exercise personal influence by cultivating networks of mutually beneficial relationships with supervisors, peers, direct reports, and even people outside the company, such as key suppliers or customers. They learn what they can do to support their network members' goals and how their network members can support their—the managers'—goals. Formal authority and professional or educational background play a little role in these exchanges of influence.

**4, b.** Many new managers assume that their job is about them, their power, and their success—but it's really about their *group* and its effectiveness and success. First-time managers can achieve a more realistic perspective about their new position by making sure they're pursuing a managerial career for the right reason: to *help their organization achieve its goals* rather than to *enhance their own image.*

**5, a.** A new team member needs more attention and guidance than more experienced members of your team. You have to pay special attention to the person until he or she learns the routine and gains familiarity with the job itself.

**6, b.** Treating people fairly may not mean treating them the same. Fairness really means finding the best ways to help *each* direct report succeed. And those ways may differ, depending on your direct reports' different situations. When you treat people differently, you're actually giving them an *equal opportunity* to do well. For example, suppose one person in your group responds to praise with immensely renewed energy, commitment, and innovativeness. You could treat him fairly—but differently—by making it a point to thank him in person at least once a week for whatever recent successes he has achieved, regardless of how big or small those successes were.

**7, b.** These characteristics make teams especially valuable when your group's work requires a combination of knowledge, expertise, and perspective that can't be found in a single individual;

when the work hinges on a large degree of interdependence among group members; or when your group faces a major challenge, such as reversing falling profitability.

**8, a.** A key defining feature of coaching is that it is a two-way partnership. That is, both parties must be willing and able to participate in it in a focused, structured way. In a business setting, coaching is more about helping someone learn and move toward his or her own, *self-identified* goals than it is about helping him or her address personal issues or imparting values, skills, or attitudes in order to reach your own objectives.

**9, b.** You need to maintain a delicate balance of encouraging employees to strengthen their problem-solving skills and drawing boundaries around what kinds of problems you will help them resolve. Being willing to solve *all* their problems prevents them from developing their own skills and autonomy. Refusing to help them solve *any* problems may make them feel unsupported and abandoned.

**10, c.** Many effective managers find that their work satisfies their need to master new abilities (achievement), shape others' performance and behavior (influence), and collaborate with respected and admired colleagues (affiliation). By contrast, effective managers don't always necessarily obtain all their direct reports' approval, nor do they necessarily have greater job security or a more clearly defined career path than other professionals do.

# To Learn More

## Articles

Goleman, Daniel. "Leadership That Gets Results." *Harvard Business Review* OnPoint Enhanced Edition (August 2000).

> A manager's leadership style strongly influences his or her organization's climate—and that climate can account for nearly a third of financial performance. The most effective managers, Goleman says, use a combination of six different leadership styles, changing the blend as circumstances dictate. Goleman describes the six styles—which include "coaching," "coercive," and "democratic"—and explains the situations for which each is most appropriate.

Goleman, Daniel. "What Makes a Leader?" *Harvard Business Review* OnPoint Enhanced Edition (November 2000).

> Goleman contends that emotional intelligence (EI)—a powerful combination of self-management and relationship skills—may have more impact on a manager's performance than his or her objective knowledge, toughness, and vision. In this article, Goleman defines the five skills that make up EI: self-awareness, self-regulation, motivation, empathy, and social skill. Maintaining that EI, unlike IQ, can be strengthened, he then offers practical suggestions for doing so.

## Books

Ciampa, Dan, and Michael Watkins. *Right from the Start: Taking Charge in a New Leadership Role.* Boston: Harvard Business School Press, 1999.

Taking on any new leadership role in the workplace—whether it's becoming a manager for the first time, joining an entirely new team, or getting a big promotion—is fraught with obstacles that can undermine your best efforts to establish authority and achieve results. As these authors point out, your actions and decisions during the first few months on the job can spell the difference between your success and failure. This book provides a practical framework to follow during your first six months in your new role—including planning that you'll want to do even *before* you take the leadership reins.

Hill, Linda A. *Becoming a Manager: How New Managers Master the Challenges of Leadership.* Boston: Harvard Business School Press, 2003.

New managers must learn how to lead others rather than do the work themselves, to win trust and respect, to motivate, and to strike the right balance between delegation and control. It is a transition many fail to make. *Becoming a Manager* traces the experiences of nineteen new managers over the course of their first year in a managerial capacity. The book reveals the complexity of the transition and analyzes the expectations of the managers, their subordinates, and their superiors. New managers describe how they reframed their understanding of their roles and responsibilities, how they learned to build effective work relationships, how and when they used individual and organizational resources, and how they learned to cope with the inevitable stresses of the transformation.

Watkins, Michael D. *The First 90 Days: Critical Success Strategies for New Leaders at All Levels*. Boston: Harvard Business School Press, 2003.

Fully a quarter of all managers in major corporations enter new leadership roles each year. Whether their assignments involve leading a work group or taking over a company as CEO, they face very similar challenges—and risks—in those critical first months on the job. How new leaders manage their transitions can make all the difference between success and failure. In this hands-on guide, Michael Watkins, a noted expert on leadership transitions, offers proven strategies for moving successfully into a new role at any point in one's career.

Watkins, Michael D. *Taking Charge in Your New Leadership Role*. Boston: Harvard Business School Press, 2001.

*Taking Charge in Your New Leadership Role* provides step-by-step guidelines for preparing for and making a successful transition to a new leadership position. By systematically focusing on four core transition management challenges—learning, influence, design, and self-management—it provides a road map for diagnosing the situation, developing priorities, and planning to get early wins. The workbook also provides comprehensive diagnostics for assessing leadership style, as well as helpful advice on building credibility, creating coalitions, and developing supportive advice and counsel networks.

## eLearning Programs

Harvard Business School Publishing. *Case in Point*. Boston: Harvard Business School Publishing, 2004.

*Case in Point* is a flexible set of online cases, designed to help prepare middle- and senior-level managers for a variety of leadership challenges. These short, reality-based scenarios provide sophisticated content to create a focused view into the realities of the life of a leader. Your managers will experience: Aligning Strategy, Removing Implementation Barriers, Overseeing Change, Anticipating Risk, Ethical Decisions, Building a Business Case, Cultivating Customer Loyalty, Emotional Intelligence, Developing a Global Perspective, Fostering Innovation, Defining Problems, Selecting Solutions, Managing Difficult Interactions, The Coach's Role, Delegating for Growth, Managing Creativity, Influencing Others, Managing Performance, Providing Feedback, and Retaining Talent.

Harvard Business School Publishing. *Coaching for Results*. Boston: Harvard Business School Publishing, 2000.

Understand and practice how to effectively coach others by mastering the five core skills necessary for successful coaching:

- Observing
- Questioning
- Listening
- Feedback
- Agreement

Through interactive role-playing, expert guidance, and activities for immediate application at work, this program helps you coach successfully by preparing, discussing, and following up in any situation.

Harvard Business School Publishing. *Influencing and Motivating Others*. Boston: Harvard Business School Publishing, 2001.

Have you ever noticed how some people seem to have a natural ability to stir people to action? *Influencing and Motivating Others* provides actionable lessons on getting better results from direct reports (influencing performance), greater cooperation from your peers (lateral leadership), and stronger support from your own boss and senior management (persuasion). Managers will learn the secrets of "lateral leadership" (leading peers), negotiation and persuasion skills, and how to distinguish between effective and ineffective motivation methods. Through interactive cases, expert guidance, and activities for immediate application at work, this program helps managers to assess their ability to effectively persuade others, measure motivation skills, and enhance employee performance.

Harvard Business School Publishing. *Leadership Transitions*. Boston: Harvard Business School Publishing, 2001.

This just-in-time performance-support resource provides you with practical insights into the challenges new leaders face during a transition. Harvard Business School professor Michael Watkins leads you through the first months in your new role. This resource provides expert advice, guidelines, and forty-one tools that will help you overcome common obstacles while you thoughtfully plan for your transition and success. Modules include guidelines for the following: diagnosing the situation you'll face in your new role; assessing your vulnerabilities and avoiding common traps; accelerating your learning and the transition process; prioritizing and planning for early wins and long-term successes; building a productive relationship with your boss; developing a strong team; creating supportive internal and external partnerships; and aligning strategy, structure, processes, skills, and group culture.

Harvard Business School Publishing. *Managing Direct Reports*. Boston: Harvard Business School Publishing, 2000.

Learn the skills and concepts you need to effectively manage direct reports and be able to apply these techniques immediately to your own situation. Through interactive practice scenarios, expert guidance, on-the-job activities, and a mentoring feature, you will learn and practice how to:

- Understand direct reports' expectations
- Manage a network of relationships
- Delegate along a continuum

Pre- and post-assessments and additional resources complete the workshop, preparing you for more productive direct report relationships.

Harvard Business School Publishing. *Managing Virtual Teams*. Boston: Harvard Business School Publishing, 2000.

This program will prepare you to successfully work with and lead a virtual team. You will understand the four factors that make up an efficient and effective virtual team:

- Great people
- Effective communication
- Appropriate technology
- A shared vision and process

Through interactive role-playing, expert guidance, and activities for immediate application at work, this workshop will help you understand and improve your ability to work and communicate through virtual channels. Pre- and post-assessments and additional resources complete the workshop, preparing you to lead a virtual team.

# Sources for Becoming a New Manager

The following sources aided in development of this topic:

Blanchard, Ken. *Situational Leadership*. Escondido, CA: Blanchard Training and Development Inc., 1994.

Ciampa, Dan, and Michael Watkins. *Right from the Start: Taking Charge in a New Leadership Role*. Boston: Harvard Business School Press, 1999.

Cohen, A. R., and D. L. Bradford. *Influence Without Authority*. New York: John Wiley & Sons, 1990.

Goleman, Daniel. "Leadership That Gets Results." *Harvard Business Review* OnPoint Enhanced Edition (August 2000).

Goleman, Daniel. "What Makes a Leader?" *Harvard Business Review* OnPoint Enhanced Edition (February 2000).

Hersey, Paul, and Kenneth H. Blanchard. "Life Cycle Theory of Leadership." *Training & Development Journal* (May 1969).

Hill, Linda A. *Becoming a Manager: Mastery of a New Identity*. Boston: Harvard Business School Press, 1992.

Hill, Linda A. "Becoming the Boss." *Harvard Business Review* (January 2007).

Hill, Linda A. "Exercising Influence." Case Note 9-494-080, Harvard Business School, May 31, 1994.

Hill, Linda A. "What It Really Means to Manage: Exercising Power and Influence." Case Note 9-400-041, Harvard Business School, February 15, 2000.

Hill, Linda A., and Maria T. Farkas. "A Note on Building and Leading Your Senior Team." Case Note 9-402-037, Harvard Business School, Revised June 6, 2002.

Hirschorn, L. *Managing in the New Team Environment: Skills, Tools, and Methods*. Reading, MA: Addison-Wesley Publishing Company, 1991.

Kotter, John P. "What Leaders Really Do." *Harvard Business Review* OnPoint Enhanced Edition (February 2000).

Watkins, Michael. *Taking Charge in Your New Leadership Role*. Boston: Harvard Business School Publishing, 2001.

# Notes

# Notes

# Notes

# Notes

# Notes

# How to Order

Harvard Business Press publications are available worldwide from your local bookseller or online retailer.

You can also call:
1-800-668-6780

Our product consultants are available to help you 8:00 a.m.– 6:00 p.m., Monday–Friday, Eastern Time. Outside the U.S. and Canada, call: 617-783-7450.

Please call about special discounts for quantities greater than ten.

You can order online at:
www.HBSPress.org